FRAGMENTS:

A Post-Traumatic Paradigm

K.D. Roche

Edited by Lizz Alezetes

Dedicated to my darlin' Mariah Lee,
for loving every fragment of me

and kicking my ass in the direction of my dreams

A NOTE FROM THE AUTHOR

A key to understanding this book is a basic understanding of how trauma affects the brain. Trauma affects multiple parts of the brain, including the prefrontal cortex, the part of the brain responsible for reasoning and language. It also affects the limbic system where the amygdala is located. The amygdala is responsible for emotions and the fight or flight mode that occurs when adrenaline is released. "The amygdala stores the visual images of trauma as sensory fragments, which means the trauma memory is not stored like a story, but by how our five senses were experiencing the trauma at the time it was occurring. The memories are stored through fragments of visual images, smells, sounds, tastes, or touch."[1] When people experience trauma, the amygdala is triggered, which may shut down the prefrontal cortex, impeding the ability to logically process the trauma. The memories surrounding the trauma become fragmented and jumbled, and they do not follow a logical, linear storyline in the brain.

Trauma alters the way that the brain processes memory and emotions and forever changes the paradigm in which a person views the world around them. Children are very resilient, and they adapt to survive in their environment. A child who experiences severe abuse learns to dissociate—or remove themselves from a traumatic experience that the brain cannot logically process. When extreme trauma occurs on a regular basis, a child lives in a constant dissociative state that preserves them throughout the abuse but makes it difficult or even impossible for them to be fully present, even when they are in a safe environment.

My intention in writing this book is not to tell my story for you to learn what happened to me, but to tell my story in a way that helps you understand how my mind adapted to survive. My brain did not develop normally or alter because of a traumatic event. My brain developed to endure severe ongoing trauma because it never knew anything else.

The title of this book is not the only thing you will find fragmented. Everything from the format to the content itself is written to help you understand how a complex trauma survivor remembers and processes information—in a very fragmented, sensory, and non-linear way.

The only thing that was consistent in my childhood was chaos. Everything was always changing—where I lived, where I went to school, what I was and wasn't allowed to do, even the name that I was called. Because there was no consistency or structure in my life, there was no foundation on which to build my memories. My memories are shared with you just the way they are stored in my own brain—*as I experienced them*. My hope is that reading my experiences through the lens of my post-traumatic paradigm brings you understanding, patience, and grace as you encounter survivors of all kinds of trauma.

All names, locations and other identifying information has been changed for safety and privacy reasons.

- K.D. Roche

A SPECIAL NOTE
ABOUT THE COVER PHOTO

A note from the photographer, who is a dear friend of mine:

This photo is called "Hidden in Plain Sight"

The picture on the cover photo was taken when I was feeling helplessly alone within the invisible elements of my deep pain. Yet, seeing this little bumblebee come alive through macro photography gave me the ability to see that my story and hidden battles are just as important as the pollen on his tiny legs. Healing is not linear, rather it is unique to each and every person that bravely enters through its doors and for me, creative outlets like photography have become a catalyst for thriving!

Jessa Dillow Crisp

www.jessacrisp.com

FOREWORD
BONNIE MARTIN, LPC

As a psychotherapist, my area of expertise is developmental trauma. I don't know when exactly my career veered onto this road, walking with survivors of profound human suffering, but, as Robert Frost so beautifully observed, taking the path less traveled by has made all the difference. The path of developmental trauma has all the markings of the path of PTSD: the re-experiencing, often without warning; the avoidance and numbing to cope with stressful reminders; and the ever-present hypervigilance that will not allow the body nor the mind a minute of rest. Where developmental trauma path diverges is the debilitating shame at the core of the survivor's belief system. This is not the fleeting type of shame one feels over a regretful action, but rather shame becomes one's identity. The survivor of developmental trauma believes that the feelings of shame and unworthiness and unlovableness from abuse and neglect actually mean that he/she is shameful, unworthy and unlovable. For the survivor of developmental trauma, there is the absence of a pre-trauma personality. There is a way forward, but the path is fraught with pitfalls, obstacles and setbacks. Sometimes darkness closes in and there appears to be no path at all. In the pages that follow you will find one person's courageous journey to keep finding the light, to keep finding the path, to keep finding their way. And in doing so, they keep finding themself. Loved. Worthy. Accepted. Just as they are. Just as they had been all along.

~ Bonnie Martin, LPC

TABLE OF CONTENTS

A Note from the Author   i

A Special Note About the Cover Photo   v

Foreword by Bonnie Martin, LPC   vii

Blackbird   1

Losing Kate, Part I   13

Losing Kate, Part II   17

Losing Kate, Part III   25

Losing Kate, Part IV   47

Losing Kate, Part V   71

Losing Kate: Part VI   91

Losing Kate, Part VII   105

Acknowledgements   119

Notes   123

BLACKBIRD

A man unleashes his rage on the front door—a door that hardly fits its frame, having been kicked and beat on so many times. Dad rolls over in a purple haze of dreamy incoherence. Needles on the nightstand. Black blankets to block out the sunlight of summer days. Slumber steals hours, days, weeks. The phone rings. The Boss knocks. The children cry. Oblivious, he sleeps.

Dad wakes, and it's time to turn on the amps, break out the bass, and put on a show. "Your dad's a rockstar, you know? One day we'll have a big house and a nice car, you'll see." His fingers run along the frets as he closes his eyes—once big and bright, now dull and faded like an old photograph. They used to shine when he would sing to me our favorite song before he put me to bed.

Blackbird fly, Blackbird fly
into the light of the dark black night...2

Dad's got friends over again. I always try to stay out of his way when people are over. I hold my breath and walk quickly but carefully through the house to keep from being noticed. Smoke rises from an ash tray in the center of the living room like signal smoke, drawing men and women in to join the party. Dad makes a joke and everyone laughs. He's laughing too, but only for a moment. "What're you laughing about?" he snaps, the veins in his forehead protruding as his face darkens red. Pacing around the house, he tosses clothes and clutter around,

1

covering up the small walking path we had used to wade through all of the chaos.

"Where is it?!" Dad shouts, hurling a vase against the wall, the echo of shattering glass jolting Zeus, our pit bull rescue, awake. He drops to his knees and puts his palms face-down onto the carpet. Heaving sobs of sorrow, he releases tears which seem to have been stored past their time of expiration. My muscles contract, squeezing my intestines as I stare at the broken glass. I hear Dad crying, but he's on the phone and I'm hunched over inside the fort I made beneath the coffee table in Mom's living room. "What's wrong, Daddy?" I whisper into the phone without parting my lips to speak. His voice is weak and he whimpers, "I love you, my little slug." Sirens wail into the speaker. "Just remember even if I can't tell you anymore, that I always love you."

Zeus licks my hand and I realize I am standing, not hunched under the coffee table. I still hear Dad's whimper, though. Grandma told me once that crying is good for you. That it lets the bad stuff out. But I don't think the bad stuff goes away. It seems more like a warning that bad stuff is going to happen.

I'm supposed to turn ten tomorrow, but I don't think I want a birthday.

Dad takes his time walking over to the couch, his young body hunched over like an old man, his weight resting on a dragon head cane he had whittled himself from a limb that had fallen in the yard. Taped to the coffee table is the number to the suicide hotline. He traces the numbers with his finger as if he was reading Braille. Half a second later, he nods off.

Take these sunken eyes and learn to see...

I wake up to get ready for school and notice that something is different about this morning. Dad's bedroom door is wide open, and I'm tempted to look inside (I haven't seen it since we first moved in, over a year ago). Afraid of what might happen if he catches me, I bypass his room and plod on to the kitchen and pack myself a lunch. The refrigerator reeks of spoiled food. Pinching my nose, I stare into the hollow space—nothing but discolored raw meat and an almost empty twenty-four pack of Heineken. Following the sound of muffled mumbles, I find Dad passed out on the couch in the same position I saw him in last, as if he hadn't moved all night. I tap him on the shoulder, and he squints up at me. "There's nothing for me to take for lunch and I don't have money on my lunch card."

"Well, I don't have any money," he mutters.

I board the bus with empty pockets and a backpack that is lighter than usual. The bus is rather empty, and suddenly, I realize why: parent-teacher conferences.

I hate parent teacher conferences.

"Where is your mother?" my teacher asks.

"In another state," I say.

"Well, where is your father?"

"He works nights."

"And he couldn't make it?"

"He's a hard worker and he works late," I answer, looking away.

"I see," she looks down on me. I tap the toe of my right shoe against the ground as I imagine the floor crumbling to open a hole for me to hide in.

This is why I hate parent/teacher conferences! I always feel stupid and have to make stuff up because I'm embarrassed that no one comes for me. I'm always the only kid in class by myself. I wish my teachers would just leave me alone and stop asking questions.

3

The teachers disdain me. I'm the dirt on their skin, and they want to wash me away.

When I reach the corner of my block, One-Eyed-Mike is waiting for me. He grabs me by the shoulders and digs his fingertips into my skin, leaving an impression. "Where's your dad, *Hija*?! He owes me big." His glass pupil swivels, while his other eye penetrates mine. Creepy. I focus my stare on the Celtic cross freshly tattooed on his bulging bicep.

"I d-don't know. Is-isn't he home? Di-did you ch-check the h-h-house?"

I want to cry. I know we don't have any money. Mike's fingers dig into my arm, pulling my skin tight, daring me to try and get away. We walk the block home in silence. Clenching my forearm in one hand, he bangs on the door with the other. No one answers. He releases me to go around back to climb through the kitchen window like I always do, since Dad never answers the door or remembers to unlock it before I get home. He always leaves the kitchen window unlocked, so I lift my legs over one at a time and find him leaned up against the counter, trembling.

When I tell Dad that Mike is at the front door, he seems both anxious and relieved. "Go to your room," he says.

I don't.

"Mike, *Hermano*!" Dad greets him.

"You better have good reason for being late payin' me! And you better have my money!" Mike threatens.

Dad reaches into his pockets and pulls out a wad of cash. Counting it bill by bill, he hands it over to One-Eyed Mike. My stomach growls and I silently pray he doesn't hear as I peer down the hallway to see what is going on. Mike pulls a bag of brownish powder out of his jacket and Dad says, "No Garbage this time, man. I want Snow. Give me the good stuff. I got your money from last week and more for a twenty-bag."

Still shaking, Dad picks up an empty beer can and crushes the middle, wiggling it back and forth until it snaps in half. He pours the powder into the bottom half of the can and drips a bit of water over the top. Pulling out a lighter, he heats the can from underneath and sucks the mixture up into the syringe. Running his hand over the bruises on his left arm and shoulder, he feels up his neck and injects himself.

Blackbird singing in the dead of night...

Not even a minute later, he groans and calls us to eat. Cold cereal. He pours himself a bowl. His head drops lower and lower with each bite until his face falls into his Frosted Flakes. I guess Dad's sleeping in the dining room tonight. My shoulders hunch forward, carrying the weight of my father's addiction as I walk down the hallway to my room. I know things aren't right, but I don't really understand why my dad can't come talk to my teachers. I squeeze my eyes shut to keep the tears inside. *He doesn't even know I have an A in reading. I was the only one that didn't miss a word on the vocabulary test, but he wouldn't care.* I pick Snakey (my pet rubber snake) up out of his cage. No matter how many times I move or where I go, I always take Snakey with me. Mom thinks his tank is too big but I don't care, he needs room for his rock and the big stick he likes to lay on. I hold him up and look at him. "Snakey, do you 'member that one time Dad read us a story before bed? I wish he would read to us again. I only wanted to live here because I missed him, but I still miss him. How can I miss him when he's still here?" It's a little early to go to bed, but I put Snakey back in his cage. I'm too tired to think anymore.

When I go outside to play, I see something moving in the center of the road. It's a blackbird with broken wings. I look up and see that it must have fallen from a nest directly above me in a tree branch suspended over the street. I take off my sweatshirt and swaddle the bird in it. "You'll be alright," I say.

I open the front door and hurry towards my bedroom carrying the bird under my right arm. "Hey!" Dad calls out from the couch. Before I can even respond, he nods off.

I take ten steps towards him, thankful that I can still hear his shallow breaths. His face is sunken in on either side like the prow and stern of the Titanic, his cheekbones jutting out like icebergs in the Atlantic Ocean. I place my hand on his shoulder and kiss him on the cheek. A shiver shimmies from my lips down through my spine. "I love you, Dad," I whisper and softly sing:

Blackbird fly, Blackbird fly
into the light of the dark black night...

I get a cardboard box from the garage, some gauze tape from the medicine cabinet, and set up a home outside for the wounded bird. I wrap his wing and check on him multiple times a day. After a week passes, I come home to an empty box.

Take these broken wings and learn to fly...

I couldn't stay with Dad. This older lady with really strong and stinky perfume came to our house and he got really mad and left. They asked me lots of questions that made me nervous. I didn't know what answers I was supposed to say, and I had a feeling the answers I gave were wrong by the way the stinky lady shook her head. She asked if there was someone else that I could live with.

I think my grandparents came to get me that day, but my brain is still a little fuzzy. But I do remember it was raining. I remember that lady's stinky perfume. And I remember that I forgot to get Snakey and no one would take me back to get him.

I don't like to think about all those things. They make my head hurt and they make me feel sad. I don't like to feel sad.

I like to think about the time he read me a story. I like to remember jumping on the bed playing the same Kermit the Frog song over and over. I miss the good stuff—fudgesicles for lunch, cereal for dinner, and video games alongside our five-dog pit bull crew.

Life was so easy, yet so hard. Things are different now. Most days the bad memories stay away. But it wasn't always that way.

All your life
you were only waiting for this moment to be free.

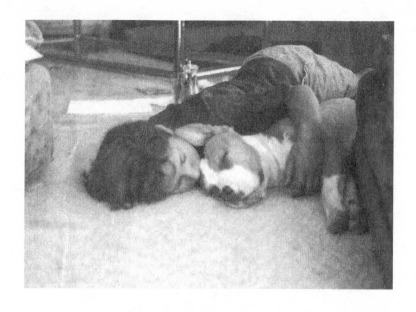

Laying with Zeus for some cuddles,
around 10 years old

Where Was Your Mother?

My mama was busy
trying to find love
somewhere between the lies
that Disney told her
and the absence
that her father showed her

She had been young
and afraid once too
her dad never in sight
never tried to fight off
the disturbing voices
of her mother's boyfriends

Boyfriends
with vile intentions
who tried to find their way
into her home
and into other places

INTERGENERATIONAL TRAUMA

I recently read a quote floating around social media that said "Trauma is the gateway drug." So much of that statement resonated with me and my experience, not only personally, but professionally. As a full-time human-trafficking field expert, I spend a lot of time with direct service providers who serve survivors of sexual assault, physical violence, psychological manipulation and other compounded traumas. It is my experience that many victims who have experienced abuse by the hands of a family member or primary caretaker have other family members, often including the perpetrator, who have also experienced similar childhood trauma.

When a person does not actively work to acknowledge and heal from their own trauma, that trauma can manifest itself through substance abuse, mental disorders, issues with emotional attachment, and/or the repeating of unhealthy behavioral patterns.

A parent who is experiencing domestic violence at the hands of a partner may not be able to tend to the needs of their child if they are constantly in a state of hypervigilance and survival. A caretaker who has not addressed their own traumatic experiences may find extreme difficulty with acknowledging and validating the experiences of their dependents.

Irreparable Holes

An absent father
in the heart of their own child
leaves a dad-shaped hole

LOSING KATE, PART I

Once Mom had quit using drugs, Dad stopped coming around. Not that we saw him much anyway. It had been a year since Mom broke the news that we were moving to a new state with her boyfriend, Alan. I didn't even get to finish first grade. She said I should be happy I got an extra two weeks of summer, but I wanted to go to the pool with my friends. Now I would have to ride in a plane to go visit Grandma and Grandpa and the rest of my family. *I hope Daddy comes to see me.*

I liked Alan. I thought he was a good guy. He was handsome and funny, and he would squat down to the ground to talk to me. I liked that. He took me to the park and taught me how to rollerblade. Mom said when they got married, he would be my stepdad. I didn't know what a stepdad was, but I knew that I missed having a dad since my daddy stopped coming to see me. It made me sad that I didn't get to hang out with him anymore. He was super cool because he had dreadlocks and played guitar. He called me slug because I was always slow at doing everything. When he did come see me, like on my birthday, he'd open his arms out and say, "Come on! Give me a big slug hug!" which made me laugh.

Alan never gave me a nickname. He was nice to my mom most of the time, but one time he made her cry and called her bad names. When he kept yelling at her, she ran into the kitchen and threw all our plates to the floor. It scared me when they broke. It scared the cats too. She said she was sorry, and everything was her fault and then he bought her flowers.

I'm glad Mom promised to let me fly back to see my grandparents, Aunt Lisa, and my cousins. I didn't like all the yelling, and Grandma made the best strawberry cupcakes.

Butterflies fly around in my stomach as soon as I get on the plane. It's my first time ever flying alone. I feel like a grown-up even though I am nervous. Not many seven-year-olds fly by themselves. I straighten up to make myself as tall as possible. The two and a half-hour flight seems like five minutes as daydreams of summer fast-forward me to Grandma's house.

My eyes search the crowd for Grandma—a tall, slender woman with kind eyes. I spot her waving and run to greet her with a big hug. I miss seeing her often like I used to. We walk to the parking garage. My cousin Joe waits for us in the car. As soon as I open the door, he crawls over the back seat, wrapping his arms around my neck. He is the same age as me. Well, two months younger, but he's always been shorter and smaller. We laugh and sing songs the hour-long drive home from the airport. Grandma makes us stop singing "This is the Song that Never Ends." She says it makes her head hurt. She does not like Lambchop or her sing-along-songs.

The dogs greet us with happy barks, and Aunt Lisa and Uncle George spread open their arms for hugs. Aunt Lisa seems so much happier since she married Uncle George two years ago. I had never met any of her previous husbands, just Joe's real dad and Uncle George, but the family says they like Uncle George best. They say he's a hard worker. I like him better too. He's a lot nicer than Joe's dad. Joe's dad always yelled at us and hardly came home, and neither Joe nor I have seen him since he and Aunt Lisa got divorced. Uncle George is different. He gives us ice cream, takes us to Chuck E. Cheese's, and lets us watch movies.

Instead of yelling if we do something wrong, he just helps us get it right the next time. Joe even calls him "Dad" sometimes.

A family trip to Chuck E. Cheese's,
about 10 years old

Didn't Anyone Know He Was a Bad Guy?

He wasn't a hell-raised, drug-crazed,
hard, intimidating or tattooed man
as many might imagine

He was more like
your Sunday school teacher
the barber, mailman or dentist

He was your best friend's brother
your girlfriend's lover
anyone other than the guy you'd suspect

LOSING KATE,
PART II

Seven. The age of popsicles. The age of slumber parties. The age of pretend.

After dinner, Grandpa makes a bed on the floor for us kids to sleep on. He always sets us up in the living room so we can fall asleep watching movies. Everyone is asleep, but the Lion King isn't over yet. I roll over and feel a hairy arm touch mine. My eyes want to open but fear demands that they remain closed. *Who is lying next to me?*

I yawn and readjust, hoping to deter the hand that grazes me intrusively. I pretend as if I am waking. Uncle George smiles at me.

"I need to go to the bathroom." I get up, walk to the bathroom, and close the door behind me, but the doorknob turns and the door pushes open.

"Shhhh," he says, "everyone is sleeping."

He closes the door behind him and turns the lock. I don't speak, but I am screaming loudly inside. No words escape my mouth, only tears from my eyes. His hands invade my body. His actions suffocate my soul. There is blood on my clothes—stains that will be tossed and forgotten. But the pain, fear, and memories forever stain the paradigm through which I view the world.

"You don't want anyone to know what a naughty girl you are. If they know what *you* did, they'll be disgusted with you.

Better you don't say a word, unless you want to be punished."
He grabs me and I jerk away from him. He laughs. "This isn't
even the beginning, little girl. Now stop actin' like you didn't ask
for it. You think you can just sleep on the floor right in front of
me? You think I've been playin' games with you, buyin' you toys
and candy expectin' nothing from you in return? Grow up! You
wanted me. You *still* want me." *I don't understand. What did I
do wrong? What did I say to him? Did I want it? NO! I never
said...but I* did *ask him to play games with me. I* did *ask him to
buy me candy.*

"Shhhh," he says, "shhhhh. Everyone is sleeping."

My soul slept that night. In fact, it hibernated for the next
nine years.

*Saved from my childhood:
My treasure box and a favorite stuffed animal*

Why Didn't You Say Anything?

See, I loved him once too
before he ruined my favorite cartoon
interrupting it
with unwelcome advances

I was silenced by fear
I knew innately this wasn't right
but even at seven years old
he said I was responsible
and if an adult says it, it must be true

A drawing done while processing
trauma memories as an adult

WHAT ARE WE TEACHING OUR CHILDREN?

As adults, we teach children to beware of strangers and how to respond if a stranger approaches or touches them. But do we teach them that sometimes, good people do bad things? Do we teach them that family, close friends, and trusted adults can sometimes hurt us?

According to the Crimes against Children Research Center, only 10% of children who suffered sexual abuse were violated by an unknown perpetrator; the other 90% knew their abuser. And in approximately 30% of child sexual abuse cases, the perpetrator was a family member.[iii]

I didn't get kidnapped, so I didn't scream. A stranger didn't touch me—a family member did. I was taught that when an adult in charge tells you to do something, you should listen. According to what I had been taught, I did the right thing when I followed him when he asked me to, even when I didn't feel right about it.

It is important that we teach our children that it is okay to say "no" even to adults that we love. I practice this with my daughter by allowing her to practice saying "no." I then have her ask herself the following questions out loud:

1) Can it hurt me or someone else?
2) Does it make me feel uncomfortable?
3) Is it something I need help with?

If Grandma asks for a kiss and she doesn't want to give her one, I teach her that it is *her* body and *she* can choose what she is and isn't comfortable with. If someone is tickling her and she wants them to stop, they are expected to honor the word "no." If they don't, she knows to tell me or another trusted adult. I recommend reading child appropriate (3-10 years) books on body, boundaries and communication. You can find a list of these on www.isaidno.info I also recommend the book *Sex Trafficking Prevention* by Savannah Sanders for adults to become informed on ways you can help prevent child abuse and sex trafficking.

Hope Deferred

Hope deferred makes the heart sick

Lack of oxygen restricts
the

        pump

            pump

                  pumping
of her heart

How long
will she wait?

A light
in her eyes
fixed and dilated

Stethoscope over chest
confirms silence

Two fingers
pressed
on the neck

Tick-tock

Who calls the clock
when hope dies?

LOSING KATE,
PART III

Nine. The age of friendship bracelets. The age of storytelling. The age of catching caterpillars.

I step off the plane and hug Grandma, breathing in the familiar scent of her homemade laundry detergent. I can't wait to see my cousins. I hope Uncle George won't be there when we arrive. The dogs bark, running in circles. The clicking of their little paws prancing on the tile welcomes us in as we arrive. Aunt Lisa and Uncle George stand up from the couch, stretching out their arms. Uncle George whispers in my ear as he leans in for a hug, "Don't you worry, hun, we've got all kinds of plans for you kids this summer." My stomach turns as I swallow the memories of the years before.

"Joe!" I run to greet him. He looks the same, tiny build and straight blonde hair. He stares at me. I hug him with both arms, but his body remains stiff. *Something is not right.*

Grandpa makes us a bed on the floor in the living room as he always does. I ask him if I can have my own sleeping bag. We are watching Cinderella. "I hate this movie!" Joe says. I'm pretty sure we are the only ones awake. I close my eyes. Cinderella is singing:

A dream is a wish your heart makes
when you're fast asleep

In dreams you will lose your heartaches
whatever you wish for, you keep

Have faith in your dreams and someday
your rainbow will come smiling through
No matter how your heart is grieving
if you keep on believing
the dream that you wish will come true[iv]

I wish for more popsicles, more movies, and more time with just me and Joe. I wish for sunshine and horses without Uncle George. Everyone else is asleep. Everyone—except for Uncle George. He walks into the living room and waves for Joe and me to follow him. *Why does he want both of us? Has he touched Joe before too?* I really don't want to go with him, but I am afraid to refuse. We follow him into the office, and he closes the door. I clench my eyelids tightly and hold my breath. My ears feel plugged up as I try to brace myself for what I know is coming.

I wait.

For my clothes to be discarded. For the intrusive hand.

One one-thousand. Two one-thousand...ten one-thousand.

I open my eyes.

There's a computer desk in the corner.

Uncle George is sitting at a computer desk in a chair, next to Joe.

"You know where you are going?" he asks.

"Got it," says Joe.

"Good. You've been working with me almost two years now and I expect you to remember what I taught you. Stay in control and give them exactly what they want."

A picture drawn as art therapy;
the treasure box is the same as the one
from the photo in Losing Kate, Part II

The Floor

I want to wear the darkness
like a weighted blanket
heavy
on my shoulders

It's pulling me

       down

             down

                    down

until
I become one
with the floor

I am the floor

I cannot feel
you stepping on me
heavy

You cannot hurt me
or break me

Hide the light
I don't want to see—
I can't feel—

the light
on my shoulders

The darkness
the blanket

it helps me

melt

      melt

            melt

like crayons
on a blistering day
that won't color anymore

Hide the sun
don't let it shine on me

in the dark
I cannot see

Hiding
escaping
becoming

the floor

Don't flip the switch—
please—don't remind me

that this is real

        I am real

            he is real

He's a dream
a nightmare

He lifts his heel
but
I'm not real

I am the floor

And the floor
won't crack
or scream

The floor
won't cry

the floor
doesn't care
about your dirty boots

Grooming Joe

My cousin, a boy, was younger than I,

for years was a victim—I watched him cry.

His stepfather trained him after breaking him down,

he raised him a pimp, well-respected in town.

I watch silently as Joe sits down at the computer. I'm just relieved that Uncle George hasn't touched me.

What does he mean give them exactly what they want? Who? What has Joe been doing working with Uncle George? I thought Uncle George was a ranch-hand and Aunt Lisa has been homeschooling Joe?

He closed the door.

It is coming. It has to be coming.

He closed the door.

"We're going to teach you a game." Uncle George smiles. "All you have to do is exactly what we tell you and there won't be any problems." *We?! So Joe is in on this now, too?*

Joe maneuvers the mouse, typing various things into the computer. I notice the press-on tattoos on his hand. He's wearing the red monster truck shirt I got him that was too big last year. The screen pops up. TEEN CHATROOM. Joe creates a familiar screen name "2young4u." Immediately the computer screen is filled with five or six pop-up chats. My heart is knocking hard on my chest.

"Hey, baby, age/sex/location?"

"9, female, Wyoming"

"Is 45 too old?"

"45 is perfect."

He's obviously done this before. He responds to the messages robotically without thought. His eyes are glassy and lifeless, like a fish at the market.

"How young?"

"9 too young?" Joe responds.

"Is 55 too old?"

"55 is perfect."

"Do you have pictures?"

"I can take some."

Uncle George is smiling. "Ok, kiddo, we're going to take some pictures." First he snaps a couple of me just standing there. "Smile," he says. A tear forms in my left eye. I wipe it away before he notices. He takes pictures of me in my t-shirt and underwear in all sorts of sitting and standing positions.

Joe is still typing away at the computer. "Alright, George, they want the pictures."

"Alright, honey, you can put your clothes back on now."

He has pictures. What is he going to do with my pictures? Why did he make me do those things?

Uncle George removes the memory card from the camera and inserts it into the computer. I stand behind my cousin and read the multiple chats on the computer screen. "Can I see a picture?" one person asks.

"Sure," Joe types, "as long as you are sure you don't mind that I'm only 9."

"I don't mind. I like it."

Joe emails a picture of me to this stranger. "Can I go to the bathroom?" I ask, hoping to escape the room, even if only for a moment.

"No. I want you to read everything Joe types. You need to learn how to do this."

The stranger asks, "Have you ever had sex before?"

Joe types, "Yes."

"And you liked it?"

"I liked it," Joe types.

"Mmm, bad girl!" the stranger replies.

The words Joe types give me a stomachache. I can feel more tears coming and I pray they will stay inside. I don't like the way Uncle George smiles like he's happy when I cry.

I remember the first time. It was here. In that bathroom. He told me I would like it, but I didn't like it. I hated it. I still hate it. I hate that bathroom. I hate Uncle George. I hate this room. I hate those pictures. I hate myself.

Grandma says hate is a bad word. I know I am bad because I can feel the hate.

"Send me more pictures. Less clothes this time."

Joe sends the pictures.

I don't sleep all night. Instead, I am forced to stay awake reading messages in a chatroom. Messages that make me feel dirty. Messages that make me feel like an object. Messages that make me feel heavy. Heavy like when Zeus sits in my lap too long, except everywhere.

On the computer Joe's words are my words. Except they aren't. He types for me everything I don't want to say. He lets the people messaging him tell him what to do. They think they are talking with me, but my cousin is the one in the chatroom.

"Are you alone?" a stranger asks.

"No," Joe types, "My cousin is here, too."

"Boy or girl?"

"Boy"

"How old is he?"

"He's nine too."

"Mmm you're a dirty girl. I want you to have sex with him and take pictures. Then send them to me," says the stranger.

Joe looks at Uncle George. "Do it. I'll type."

Little Boy Puppet

The perpetrator
once a scared little boy
who couldn't cry
because that's what sissies do
and people might think
he was gay

For oppression
of women and girls
I will cry
But also for boys
who are taught to hide

to hide the abuse
and pretend it's not there
to hate only themselves
and to silence despair

No child should be born to bear
the sins of their ancestors
no child is born
preying on the innocent

The pain, the fear, the silence
pump sets of reps
building muscles that repeat
the only motions
that they've been taught

Does Anybody Hear the Boys Who Cry?

Where are the men, moral and grown
who will take a boy up by the hand
and tell him he's not alone

That it's okay to cry
it's okay to feel the pain

To crave the strength of a full-grown man
as a boy frozen in fear—

this

is real

"Please don't make me do this," I beg. Uncle George turns around in his chair and slaps me across the face. Everything in my face feels numb. I wish my whole body felt numb.

My body hurts. I can't think anymore. All I want to do is sleep. Uncle George throws me a wet washcloth. "Here," he says, "Clean yourself with this." He sends the pictures to the stranger.

"Who took these?" the stranger asks.

"My uncle did."

"Really? He's ok with it? Do you have sex with him too?"

"Yes."

"You should have sex with him too. Record it and take pictures. I want to see it."

Uncle George always does what the men in the chatroom want. When they want pictures, he takes them; videos, he shoots them.

I don't even know how I feel anymore.

I feel how he tells me to feel. I do what he tells me to do.

I can't think for myself, act for myself, or even dress myself anymore.

I have lost myself to a role that I didn't audition for.

The next night is the same. Joe types. Uncle George watches, delegating if necessary. Uncle George starts calling me "slave." He doesn't call me "honey" or by my name anymore, just "slave." Joe calls me "slave" too. Like he doesn't know me anymore. Like we were never close. He looks at me with disgust and talks to me like I'm a bad dog. *What happened? I used to have fun with Joe. We laughed together and played games. He stood up for me when I got made fun of and made me feel special. Something is wrong with him now and it scares me.*

I get in the shower, turning the knob almost all the way to hot. I scrub my body vigorously with the rough side of a dish sponge. *Maybe if I scrub hard enough I will feel clean again.*

I sit in the corner on the bathroom floor and cry. *I still feel dirty; nothing makes me feel clean.*

My skin stings.

My body is sore.

My mind is numb.

Rise Up for Justice

I couldn't tell you the number of times I've been asked,
"Could anyone have made a difference?"
And I know what you are looking for,
I know what you mean,
and I know the answer that you want me to say.
I'd like to say "yes," that the pediatrician
could have questioned the third UTI I had in a month.

My teacher could have asked
why I was so tired that I slept through every class.
I'm sure event security saw the men
come and go
from the RV.

But we've been taught by society
to mind our own business
because our concerns might not be validated
and the fear of being invalidated
has a way of paralyzing us
because silent
is not as uncomfortable as wrong.

America, home of the brave,
So brave in fact
we avoid what makes us uncomfortable

Afraid to leave our phones at home.
What would we do if we had to hold a real conversation
with someone we didn't know
or sit in uncomfortable silence?

See the problem was not
that no one knew
what was going on.
The problem
was not even that no one believed me.
The problem
was that nobody wanted to acknowledge there was a
problem.

I wake up early and sneak outside to call Mom. We don't normally talk much while I'm visiting Wyoming. She figures no news is good news and I figure that there's not a whole lot to say. Sometimes she will call to ask Grandma if everything is going okay, but we don't usually talk to each other.

"Hey Mom, it's me."

"Hi honey. Is everything okay?" As soon as the words come out of her mouth, I can't speak. I try to form words but only sobs come out. "What's wrong, baby?"

"It's Joe. And Uncle George. They keep making me do things I don't want to do."

"That's just part of growing up, baby."

"No, Mom. I mean, bad things. Dirty things."

"I know what you're talking about. I read your journal last summer."

"What?!"

"I read everything. I wasn't going to embarrass you by saying anything. After you came home from Wyoming, you left your journal open on your desk in your room. I read what happened. You are just getting older. Men can't help themselves, they're curious. Your Uncle George didn't mean any harm by what he did. Joe's getting older too, so I'm not surprised now that he's giving you a little attention. His hormones are probably just a little crazy. It's a normal part of growing up, honey. Boys are sexual. It only gets worse as they get older. You'll be okay. It'll help you to grow up a little. But listen, I have to go. Don't worry so much. Try to go with it. It makes everything easier and more enjoyable. I'll see you in August!"

She read my journal?! How could she know this was happening and not say anything?! Why would she make me come out here to visit if she knew?!

Normal?! Did this happen to her too? I don't understand.

41

Too Close to Home

And her mama, she was pretty too
but sometimes she didn't know what to do
because hurting people
hurt people
when they strive
just to survive

Is my whole life going to be like this? I don't think I can do this.
Suddenly, I feel dizzy. My stomach tightens and I bend over, getting sick all over the flowerbeds.

"What are you doing out here?" Uncle George yells, startling me to a standing position. I stand in front of the phone, hoping he won't see it.

"I felt sick, so I came out to get some fresh air."

"Get inside. Now!"

Grandma is sitting in her recliner in the living room. "Are you okay, sweetie? You look a little pale. You're way too thin!" She shakes her head while she looks me up and down. I don't like it when people do that. It makes me feel gross. "You know if you don't stay healthy you won't be able to do the things you love, like ride horses at the ranch. Sit down, I'll fix you something to eat." *I don't want anything to eat.*

I'm sick.

I keep hearing the words from that phone call.

I didn't know

    they would

        repeat
        (repeat)
        ((repeat))

        for years
            to come.

Aren't you ⭐ supposed
to be strong for me
Just be my mom.
Take care of me and
love me enough to
help me and not
just stand back and
let me get hurt.
Part of me wants
to hate you right
now. Who do I have
anymore. I'm in this
alone — I've got God,
but you don't even
care if I make it.
They want something
better for me here.
Why don't you want
something better
for me?

Mom, how ⭐ did you know and let me shit go? Why did not say anything? I'm angry. I know that you have problems too. I love you still. But I hate that you let this happen.

An excerpt from a journal entry,
written when I was around 14 years old

Why Did You Keep Going Back?

I remember crying
"please don't make me go
they make me so uncomfortable"
and you said
"I know
that's normal
boys will be boys"

So I picked up a set of lingerie
and I put away my toys

LOSING KATE,
PART IV

The summer of twelve is here. The age of acne. The age of loud music. The age of a first kiss.

"Mom, I don't want to go to Wyoming this year. Please don't make me go. Can't I stay home?"

"Sweetie, that's ridiculous. You have to spend time with your dad's side of the family, and you love riding horses with your Aunt Lisa! This is the only time you see them besides the three weeks you spend there for Christmas vacation."

"I don't want to go." *I do want to ride horses, but not if it means staying in the same house as Uncle George and Joe!*

"Well, you're going. And you'll have a great time."

My nerves keep my stomach in constant distress. I throw up every day for at least a week before leaving.

I don't eat.

I can't eat.

Maybe if I don't eat, I'll die.

Then it will be over.

I cry myself to sleep every night and pray to die. I board the plane. My body trembles involuntarily and goose bumps rise up on my arms and legs. The stewardess asks me if I am alright. I nod my head, though part of me wants to ask her if it is possible for me to get off of the plane. As the plane takes off, my anxiety bubbles like a volcano from the base of my stomach until the little bit of breakfast I managed to eat erupts from my mouth into the aisle. The people around me are holding their noses and gagging.

God, I am disgusting. Everyone thinks so.

No one wants me around.

Just Uncle George. Just Joe.

When I arrive, I don't see Grandma. I sit and wait for her. Large hands press down on my shoulders from behind. "You ready, little slave?" I feel the hot breath of his whisper in my ear. A chill goes through my body and suddenly I am cold again. I stand up.

"Daddy missed you," he says.

"Is this your dad?" the stewardess asks me. I nod. *Why can't I just say no?*

We walk out to the parking garage. Joe is waiting by the car. He's taller than he was last year, but he's just as skinny and still shorter than me. "You're gonna have lots of fun this summer, little slave." Uncle George says with a laugh. Joe leans his back against the truck and stares down at me, but he doesn't say anything. His stare is focused, and his eyes seem crueler than the year before. I look away and scratch my arm. When I lift my head back up, he's still staring in the exact same spot.

"Joe?! Are you okay?!" My head cocks slightly to the right and my fear *of* him turns into fear *for* him. "Joe!!"

"No! Please don't!!" he jumps, as if startled by his own voice.

Uncle George grunts and then slings my duffle bag against Joe's chest. "Boy, you better get your shit together!" He climbs into the cab of the truck, turning the keys. The ignition rumbles and Joe steps on the tire to push the bag up over the rails and into the bed of the truck.

We Can Do Better

Validate feelings
of young men who need support
Relieve them of shame

A Message for Boys

Be gracious, son
with yourself
You are the boy
who deserved to be held
and protected
and that doesn't make you weak

You can grow into a man
learn right from wrong
and be strong
I know you can

Your courage, it comes
from integrity upheld
In living your life
you can expel
the shame of the past
corruption, abuse,
the intolerable acts done by both women and men
You can lift your head up in confidence again

We drive over an hour before I realize that we aren't going to Grandma's house. "Where are we going?" I ask.

"We're going to the ranch house."

"Aren't we going to Grandma's for a few days first?"

"No." Uncle George says, "She's sick. Worse than she was before. Some days she can't remember who her own kids are. Bringing you to see her would just confuse her more. The doctors say she has Alzheimer's. It'll only get worse. She probably already forgot you." *Is she going to die? Will I ever get to see her again?* I try to forget the way things were. I know they'll never be the same. Staring out the window, I try to focus on the fields, the shops, the trees—anything but Grandma. Still I cannot forget her gentle voice, "Honey, I love you," she told me every day. *I know she does.* She would tuck my little flyaway wisps of hair behind my ears. *She couldn't forget me. She wouldn't forget me . . . would she?*

Uncle George stops at a convenience store and fills the truck with gas. When he gets back in the car, he throws me two ice cream sandwiches. "Eat these, little girl. Nobody wants to be with a scrawny woman."

We drive another hour or so. I keep hearing Uncle George's words. *Nobody wants to be with a scrawny woman.*

But I'm not a woman. I am twelve years old. And I don't want to be with anybody. I just want to be alone. I just want to see Grandma. I just want to disappear.

I am Ana Mia Nervosa
My Full Name is Anorexia/Bulimia Nervosa
But most just refer to me as Ana or Mia

I will make you feel complete
I will make you feel whole
I will make you happy
With me you will achieve all of your Goals
with me and only with me
Everyone will see your perfection
They will see that girl with direction
In her life

With Me and only with Me
You will be perfect
For the first time in your life
You will be in control

I will make you beautiful
I will make you flawless
I will make you envied
By all

All of your problems will be solved
Once you take my hand
Others will wish to be like you
Once you have my brand
I see you have come to me for direction
Thanks for riding aboard this train
I know that I promised you perfection
But what I give to you is pain

You thought that I would give to you
A great deal of control
But what you did not realize is
That is what I stole

I have secluded you from the outside world
But you have yet to realize
I have taken you from your closest friends
Much to your demise

Who now do you turn to
When the world has left you standing alone?
Not to your friends or family
For I stole them, you now have none

52

So where were you when the ones that you love
Slowly drifted away?
Too busy with me, your new friend, Mia
Much to their dismay

You were too lost in finding perfection
Too lost in your new sense of control
Too lost in my faulty direction
And it has finally taken its toll

You're beautiful now
Was it worth it?
You're perfect now
The world knows it
You're thin now
And you're envied for it

But you have lost those that you love
You are consumed with me
No time for fun
No time for friends and family
But you are thin
You win

Isn't this what you wanted?
Isn't this what life is about?
Isn't it great, now that you're perfect?
Well I'm sorry, it's too late now

You sought to find control
You sought to find perfection
Well I took you for a stroll
And you fell for my deception

You only wish now that you could leave me
But it's too late
Because without me you couldn't breathe
For your life I dominate

So hang on to me
I'm your only friend
The others no longer care or understand
Reach out to me
I'm there for you
I will take your hand

A poem I wrote just after I turned 16, while still struggling heavily with an eating disorder

When we arrive at the ranch, Uncle George takes my bags, and I never see them again. He walks me to the guest house. There's a twin bed with a sheet on it and a dresser with broken drawers. Inside the drawers are some clothes—thin, sheer material in red and black and a cheerleader's uniform. There is a box in the bottom drawer. In it is a pair of handcuffs and other items. The windows are broken, and the room is decorated with pictures of horses, cowboys, coiled ropes, and horseshoes.

The carpet is dirty and there are spiders and cobwebs along the corners. The room is humid, and I can almost taste mold when I breathe. I need a deep breath of fresh air, but my lungs want to close as I hold my breath to keep from coughing. There is a box fan leaned up against the wall, circulating the musty air.

"Alright you little cum-slut, we're going to have some fun with you. After today, you won't ever forget that you're a fucking whore. I want you to always remember what you are. Just a stupid, little slut-slave that can't even think for itself. Joe's going to be your master now. You call him 'Master.' If you call him anything else, we'll beat the shit out of you. Got it?" I nod. "I'll still be around, but when I'm not, Joe owns you."

Owns me?

"And you sure as hell know you ain't gonna tell nobody about this. You get to talk when one of us tells you you can talk. Got it?"

I nod my head, even though I have lots of questions.

"Good. Now come with us. We are going to get something to eat. We have big plans for you later."

I stare down at the burger and fries in front of me. *I'm not hungry.* "I can't wait to see how this goes," says Uncle George to Joe. "I have a feeling we're going to be in business here real quick."

I push the fries around my plate with a fork. *Nobody wants to be with a scrawny woman.* Uncle George puts a twenty-dollar bill on the table, and we head to the truck.

"That's a nice horse trailer you got there, cowboy. I bet that cost you a pretty penny," a stranger remarks as Uncle George unlocks the truck.

"Yeah, it's real nice. Wasn't my check though. The perks of being the main cow-hand for a rich man."

"Must be nice." The dusty stranger looks over the trailer again.

"Like to take a look inside?"

"Sure would!" They disappear and don't come out of the trailer for ten minutes or so. When they emerge from the trailer, the stranger gives Uncle George a hard pat on the shoulder and winks at me. "I'll be seeing you a little later, darlin'." My stomach churns and I feel the urge to throw up. *I have to find a bathroom, quick. I've got to get rid of this nasty feeling in the pit of my stomach.*

Thirty minutes later, we pull in to the county fairgrounds. There are trucks and trailers parked everywhere. Horses are tied up to fence posts and every available stall is full. Lawn chairs and coolers are set up all over the place. Everyone is wearing boots and buckles and most men have a faded circle in their back pocket from where they keep their chew.

"Don't worry, slave. You'll get used to rodeo," Joe says. "People help each other out around here. Everybody's got a little something that somebody else has need of. You'll find that out real quick. Tradin' is an easier way of life."

Slave. The word triggers memories of everything Uncle George said. *I want you to always remember what you are.* I remember the warnings he gave me. My heart beats rapidly, and I suddenly feel faint. It seems that every other man who passes by is looking me up and down, giving me a nod or a wink.

"You stupid bitch! Stop shaking!" Joe yells. His hard stare reflects anger and hate. His conscience is callous, like the working hands of a roping cowboy. *What happened to my favorite cousin?*

"Hey there, cowboy!"

"Hi Pete." Joe shakes his hand. "You here to shoe the horses?"

"Yes sir," he says with a wink, looking at me like a lion hunting its prey. His hard, focused stare is directed at me and he turns his back against Joe as he takes a step closer. He bares his teeth and bites his bottom lip. I feel trapped in a den with a hungry lion. He stares into my eyes until I look down at my feet. He laughs. I know he can feel my disgust by the way he smiles when he walks away.

Joe grabs my hand and walks me to the other side of the trailer. "Pete's going to shoe the horses, and when he's done, you are going to pay him."

"But I don't have any money." My eyes scan the area. I want to run but see nothing except dirt in every direction. *Where would I go?*

"You don't need any. You just let him take you into the trailer. There's a bed in there. You do whatever he tells you to do and act like you like it. You remember what you are now, don't you? You are a sex slave. Ain't nothing gonna change about that. You are going to learn to like this. Understand?"

"Joe, please!"

"Stop it. I am not Joe to you anymore! I am your master! Don't look at me like that. Just do it."

"What did he do to you? Your stepdad is a monster! Did he rape you too?"

Before I can react, he knocks me to the ground. "You say anything like that to me ever again and I'll beat you like the worthless piece of shit you are. Now get up off the ground, slave." He says, spitting in my face. "I'm nothing like you. *I'm the one in control here!*"

Kicking the dirt, he walks over to the step that leads to the trailer door and takes a seat. His eyes don't stop watching me. I won't let him see me cry. I pick up a rock from the ground and throw it as hard as I can into the dust. For a half-second I feel better. I pick up another. Breathing heavily, I chuck it as hard as I can.

I close my eyes and remember Joe teaching me how to skip rocks. Hate and anger return with the opening of my eyes. Adrenaline is pumping through my body. My mind is filled with violent thoughts and words I've never spoken aloud.

Nothing but a Number

There's always an age of accountability
but I encourage us to really think
about the foundation
which sets this trap

of selling people
like commodities on the street
not even at a set price
but always able to be bargained down
like merchandise
that has lost its value.

Ignorance is Not Bliss for the Victimized

We must open our eyes:
these are not third world tales
This is happening *here*

In our schools
and our churches

Children

    for sale

"He's ready for you." Joe grabs my arm and shoves me up the step. The door slams shut behind me. Twenty minutes pass before the farrier steps out of the horse trailer. I pick my clothes up from the floor. My body is stiff, my skin is a jacket I've outgrown. One of the straps to my halter-top is torn and it no longer ties around my neck. I search the trailer and find a t-shirt in one of the drawers. I pull it over my head. *There must be a brush around here somewhere.* I try to comb my matted hair with my fingers.

The door swings open. It's Joe. "You have two minutes," he says. "Someone else is here to see you."

I could run or fight, but I don't have the energy. I have no idea where I would go. Home is so far away. I climb back on the bed, pull up the comforter and hide beneath the covers. I bury my head into a pillow. I close my eyes and wish I were dead. *God, where the hell are you? What have I done to deserve this?* Someone is banging on the door. *Am I supposed to tell them to come in?* The door opens. A tall, lanky man appears wearing a ballcap. His face and clothes are dirty, and he smells like horse manure. "What are you doin' under the blankets?" he snaps. "Don't you know I was comin'? Get up outta there." He spits a mouthful of chew into an empty beer can that he picked up off of the floor.

I pull the covers down a little and sit up. "How 'bout you hurry the hell up?" His red eyes are glaring at me and his right hand yanks the covers off of the bed and onto the floor. "You ain't gonna give me no problems. I'll be sure o' that!" Knocking me on my back with his forearm, he puts his weight on my chest with his knee.

I can hardly breathe, his knee presses so hard against my ribs. One hard swallow and my emotions are gone. I feel pressure against my body. His mouth moves. I know he is talking to me, but I can't hear what he is saying. I smell dirt, sweat and tobacco. "Answer me, cunt!" His fist blows against my jaw. I taste blood.

I close   my   eyes

and picture   a sunflower

staring   until   my body

becomes

the stem

stiff

tall

sun

flower

I will not

move

with the

wind

"Thanks for nothin', bitch! I guess I'll be seein' more of you since I reckon your man is gonna be wanting more of this," he says, holding up a clear bag of white powder. "You must make your family sick every time they look at you."

They did this for drugs?! Am I gonna have to do this every time they need more drugs? Every time the horses need shoeing? Every time they can't pay for something?

Sunflower

Uncle shook their hands
　　　they shoed the horses
　　　　　waived our
　　　　　fees
　　　　　　and
　　　　　　　somewhere
　　　　　　　　after that between
　　　　　　　　　my stomach and my knees
　　　Pain
pounds

through
　　　my
　　　　body
　　　　　　　　　　　　　and
　　　　　　　　　　　　　　pumps

　　　　　　　　　　　　　　　into
　　　　　　　　　　　　my
　　　　　　　　　　　　heart

　　　　suffering
invades

　　　my
　　　　mind

I close my eyes

count back from ten

and open them
to find

a barren field of dead grass   blowing in the wind.
                              I
                            focus
                          my sight

                            on
                            the
                          single
                        sunflower

        standing   tall

        the winds   awaken me

                      to the smell
                        of fall.

                        I am
                    a sunflower.
                        I am
                    a sunflower.
                        I am
                    a sunflower.

I am a sunflower
standing tall
in a barren field

blowing
in the winds
of violence

waiting
for the
the rain

rooted in the hardened ground
protected from all the pain

Rodeo days turn into rodeo weeks. We travel to many places. The names all blur together. Rodeo weeks become rodeo months. I stop keeping track of the days—it seems easier that way. I stop counting the people. "A lot" seems like a lot less than if I had to say an actual number. As the days and numbers grow longer and longer, each restless night becomes just another thoughtless motion. Each trick becomes a morbid magician, bringing death to me with each act I have no choice but to perform.

But this is not an illusion.

Or is it? The only truth I know is that I cannot trust anyone. Every imaginable person passes through the door of the trailer. Young faces and grey beards, cracked hands and painted fingernails. Business suits and cowboy boots. The county drug dealer and the county sheriff. I watch them like a movie. Each new character introduced to a scene becomes harder to see. My vision becomes increasingly blurry until I cannot see.

When each summer ends, I go back home to Mom's house. Each fall and winter break, I go back to visit Dad's family. Sometimes I get to see Grandma and Grandpa. Sometimes I get to see Dad. But usually, I just see Uncle George, Aunt Lisa, and Joe.

Sometimes I am not sure where I am at all because with Uncle George and Joe we are always traveling to new places.

We travel for rodeos
he is a country man
employed by a rancher
branding new calves
    and
    branding me
and other innocent girls
singeing our skin with an iron brand of the family initials

to let everyone know

who we belong to

I'm Not Alright

I can't have people walk behind me
without panic attacks

and get depressed every November
and December
when I remember

that holidays meant overtime
pretending all was fine

expected to be grateful
pass the ham
say why I'm thankful

look my uncle in the eyes
and smile
while Grandma slices pie

"It's so great to have the family here!"
she lifts my chin
and says
"stop moping dear"

and

life

just

carries

on

A family photo at Christmastime, when I was about 14 years old

LOSING KATE, PART V

Uncle George drives down the farm road that leads to the ranch house and I recognize where we are going. Aunt Lisa has a big meal prepared to welcome us home. Some of the people Uncle George works with are there, as well as some of the neighbors and their kids. Everyone gathers around picnic tables outside. They talk about their horses, cattle and the weather. Kids are jumping into the pool with messy faces. The older kids are playing a game of hide-and-seek.

"Look at you," Aunt Lisa says, "You hardly look fifteen! You still have lots of growing to do!" *I've got no growing to do. I have zero plans of gaining a pound or starting to look any more like a woman. I wish she would leave me alone about the way I look!*

"Come on Kate, I want to show you something!" Joe grabs me by the wrist and pulls me after him. We walk down the gravel road to one of the hay barns where three older teenage boys are waiting inside.

"You've gotta be kidding me. I didn't know you were really serious!" one of the boys says. His eyes are wide and his steps are shaky. He's smiling.

"Alright, slave, do whatever they want. If you mess up, I'll know, 'cause I'll be watching." Joe whispers. I look over at the boys. The smallest of the three is much bigger than I am. He has long, unruly hair and looks very strong for his age, probably about sixteen. The other two boys look older. Eighteen maybe. I walk inside and two of the three boys push me further back into the barn. They ask me if I'm ready, but I don't say anything.

Instead, I focus on a small sunray, shining through a tiny hole in the barnwood door.

>*How can the sun shine*
>*on the darkest day of summer?*

I close my eyes
hold my breath
and count back from ten

nine
eight
seven
        I bury the sights

six
five
four
        I bury the smells

three
two
one
        I bury the noise

I pull the lever
only in emergencies
this is not a drill

I let the wind blow
to uncover all of the tears
kept frozen inside
to preserve my own dignity,
on a day
that I might otherwise die
in shame.

I open my eyes

and

AWAKEN

the

sunflower

inside.

(Joe waits outside.)

When the three boys leave, I am too weak to stand. Joe comes back inside the barn. "Get up!" he demands. "Come around the back with me. I'll take you to the bathroom and you can clean yourself up. You look like a ho."

As I step into the shower, the water becomes contaminated with the shame of my rapists' sweat and semen on my body. The broken skin on my back stings like the broken promise Cinderella sang to me about my dreams. The dirty water drags my tears down the drain and washes them away along with all my wishes.

As soon as I turn off the shower, I hear people talking and laughing outside the door. It's the boys from the barn. They are laughing about how scared I looked when they threw me on top of the hay. *I hate them. I will never let anyone think I am scared ever again. I will show them I don't care. I will show them I can do anything without crying. I'm never crying again!* I notice my body shaking and I lay down on the bathroom floor hoping for it to stop. *They didn't hurt me.*

I dress my wounds with the same dress I use to hide my nakedness.

I cover my bruises with the same foundation I use to cover my sadness.

The damp towel is my pillow and a dry towel I took from the linen closet is a scratchy comforter. I want to sleep in the bathroom because I can lock the door.

Aunt Lisa bangs on the door. I flinch and my muscles tighten to protect me from anything that might be coming. I don't want anyone to see me in this dress. Bad things always happen to me when I wear it. Even when it's clean, it feels dirty when I put it on.

"Kate, are you still in there? Open the door!" I am relieved to hear Aunt Lisa's voice because I know I can tell her what happened. She told me once that most guys are perverts. Mom doesn't think that. She thinks guys are amazing. She always talks about how great Alan is, even when I told her that I saw him kiss a woman at our apartment complex's pool. One time, Aunt Lisa told me that a guy tried to twist her nipple when she was fifteen and she kicked him in the nuts. I know she doesn't want anyone to talk bad about her husband or her son, but she doesn't have a reason to care about those other boys.

I crack the door just enough to let her in while I hide behind it, just in case anyone else is standing inside the room. "What is going on?!" she asks, loud enough for the whole house to hear.

"Shhhh!" I whisper, afraid someone might hear. Joe will punish me if he finds out that I am telling his mom.

He scares me. When did he start scaring me as much as Uncle George?

I used to feel Uncle George behind his conscience. I could almost hear the echo of his threats to Joe. "I'll remind you exactly how to demand respect if you can't make her obedient. I'll teach you how to be scared if you can't control her with fear." But it seems like a little more of him goes away every time he calls me back to the trailer, every time he makes me call him 'Master,' every time he throws me down and kicks me with the spurs on his boots. I used to feel *my* Joe in there somewhere, even though he gets further and further away. But I can't find him anymore. There's no attachment at all when he looks at me like he never knew me. Like he never loved me. I can see the satisfaction on his face now every time he makes me call him "Master." I've never felt pain like this before. We were sidekicks, always together. We stood up for each other. He used to be my favorite person to laugh with. Now I can't even smile when he's around.

A tear slides down the side of my nose. *I miss Joe. I just miss him. I miss all the good times.* Like the time we planted marigolds in the old lady's yard who lived across the street so we could start our own business planting flowers. Like the time we sat at the bar and ordered root beers in frosted mugs. Like the time we threw water balloons over the fence at the cars and someone came to the door. We hid behind a tree when we heard Grandma cuss for the first time.

"Are you going to answer me?" she snaps, bringing me back to the present. I'm in the bathroom crying. It takes me a few seconds to remember why I'm crying. As soon as I remember I can feel it in my stomach. *I don't want to be here.*

"Hell-ooooooo?! Why are you in here? Why are you crying?!" It hasn't even been ten minutes and I've already broken the promise I made to myself that I wouldn't cry. I try to form words, but I can't find them as fast as she wants me to answer her.

The words are lost with my consciousness. I keep going away in my head.

My mind is a city.   It used to be a town,

but it keeps growing.   Every time   something bad happens
I make a new building,   put the memory inside   and lock
the door.   I am in the barn. I see them   on top of me.

"No!!" I shout.

I cover my face with my hands but leave a small space for light to
shine through between my pointer finger and my index finger. "Look
at the light" I whisper to myself like the wind,

Ten

Nine

Eight

"What light?" Aunt Lisa asks me. "What are you talking about?"

Seven

Six

Five

I look at the light

Four

Three

Two

I close my eyes

and

I am a sunflower again

"Come here, you can talk to me." I pull my knees in to my chest and take a deep breath. I interlock my fingers and place my hands on the back of my head, pushing it down slowly until my forehead is resting on my knees.

"Those boys," I try to take a deep breath but the way I am sitting makes it difficult. "Joe's friends," I continue, "They raped me." I hold my breath. *Why isn't she saying anything.* I'm afraid of her silence. *What is she going to say? Did I make a bad choice? I shouldn't have said anything.*

Nothing

could have prepared me
for her response
when I told her what happened.
The sound waves from her voice
bouncing back and forth

from the left
side of my skull   to the right.

I would hear it

again and again.

An audio-file

set to repeat her words

any time I would think about telling anyone
anything *ever again.*

79

"Rape,"

. . .

. . .

she said,

. . .

. . .

"is a **strong** word."

"You shouldn't use that word. I'm sure that's not what really happened. You know that if you say anything, you could be taken from the ranch, right? You would never be able to ride horses and it would be your own fault. You might not ever see your family again. You wouldn't do something *that selfish*, would you?"

"I won't say anything." *Even if I wanted to say anything, I wouldn't. Not because you told me not to, but because I'm not stupid anymore. Nobody gives a shit about me. I'm never trusting anyone ever again.* "Just don't let them stay the night, please."

"I won't. But you have to come out of the bathroom."

She swore she wouldn't let them stay the night, but she let them anyway. How am I supposed to trust anyone? *I can't do this. I can't let them hurt me anymore.* I walk to the liquor cabinet and drink straight from the bottle of Jack. *I'll be fine.* My face scrunches up as the whiskey burns my throat. I don't care how bad it tastes as long as I don't have to feel anything bad. Everything hurts and I don't want to cry anymore.

Joe calls me over to the pool room. The boys who raped me are in there, but now there are other guys in there too. Some of them seem like they are in their twenties, but some of the other guys are older—a lot older. Some of them even have grey hair and wrinkles on their face. *I don't want to remember this. I don't even want to know what's going to happen.* "Here ya' go, honey!" an old man shouts at me, holding up a shot glass, "This will make you feel better!" *Why are they here? What are all these old guys doing here?!*

A hand presses my shoulder from behind and I gasp with surprise. I didn't expect it. It's Uncle George. "I brought some friends over tonight for you Kate!" He smiles and whispers in my ear, "Don't get used to having a name, slave. I'm just being nice for the guests." A man in a police uniform walks into the pool room. *Oh shit! Is he going to arrest me?! No! What will happen if they take me away?! What if I never see my family again?! Am I going to go to jail?!*

He doesn't arrest anyone. He is here for sex too, just like everyone else.

I don't fight at all anymore. I just want to get it all over with as soon as I can. The alcohol makes it a little easier. I stare at a painting hung on the wall. It's a weeping willow tree by the water.

I stare

until my body

leaves the room.

<u>Lullaby</u>

Weeping willow tree
with branches that will not break
sway me calm to sleep

The next morning, when I regain consciousness, I am alone. I am completely naked, and I have a massive headache. My muscles are sore, and I have bruises everywhere. My hair smells like booze and written across my stomach in lipstick is "Fuck-whore slave." I remember the party. The guys. The cop. *No one will ever believe me if I try to tell them anything. It doesn't even matter. Mom, Aunt Lisa, the cop . . . they didn't do anything to stop it, and if they won't, no one ever will.*

I don't think I can do this anymore.

Where's that bottle of Jack?

I keep having ★ nightmares
about that ▓▓ night in
the pool room. I wake up and
feel like it has physically happened
again. I feel the feelings all
over again. I hear the music,
see them laughing, they're holding
me down, I'm crying + ▓▓
is watching. I feel hate for
him. But I hate myself for
being ▓▓ him.
What's worse is it stays with me
all day. I've never had stupid
flashbacks like this. Now all of the
sudden ~~everything~~ everything
triggers memories. ▓▓▓▓▓
looked exactly + sang exactly like
▓▓▓▓▓ When that Pastor at church
put his hand on my shoulder I
wanted to scream + cry + run
away.
    But I remember 2x this
week ~~where~~ where I really
wanted to throw up but didn't.
Those were major victories for
me, but it's hard to not feel

that ~~xxxx~~ ★ those victories don't matter when I top them off with mistakes. I am a hostage to my own humanity. I threw up again. I just want Him to take it away, but I once ~~xxxx~~ heard it said that enduring faith ~~xx~~ is better than delivering faith. Maybe He's giving me (or making me ~~xxx~~ build) ~~enduring~~ enduring faith.

A journal entry recalling the night in the pool room, 15 years old

But Those People Weren't All Involved, Right?

We all want to believe
our kids aren't the bullies,
our spouses don't purchase sex or watch underage porn,
our city officials, our law enforcement, our social workers
don't know about it
and if they did,
they would stop it.

but this epidemic is a detrimental disease
being sneezed all over the tv that you watch,
the music that you listen to,
the events you attend,
and the money you hold in your hand.

While it might be hard for you to accept,
I bet everyone reading this has touched the sleeve
of a John while shaking hands with him
or passed a pimp or someone being trafficked
at the airport, bus stop, casino, club or the mall.

Back to School

My stepdad lectures me for every "B"
but to him a "C" is completely unacceptable
It doesn't matter
if the "C" is in geometry
and my brain excels
in language, history, and art

Math and science were hard for me to grasp
but it's not for lack of trying,
I spend my lunches in tutoring
and when the bell rings
head out the door, crying.

I shove my report card
into the pocket of my hoodie
and head to the stairwell
my go-to hiding place
where I try to rid myself
of shame and disgrace.

"Trouble-maker!" kids' parents call me
"Defiant!" the teachers say
I wear black skinny jeans,
keep my hood up
and smoke cigarettes
with the seniors in the parking lot after school

I never meant to be "that stoner kid"
but the first time
Kyle offered me a puff
after we left the skate park

was the first time
I forgot that I was angry.
It was the first time I forgot
that *I hated myself*.

But the high always wore off
and eventually
I'd have to go back to the home
of everybody's favorite uncle who smelled like strong cologne
and looked like a timid, middle-aged fellow

LOSING KATE: PART VI

*At my first school dance, with my first boyfriend,
my first heartbreak*

Sweet Sixteen. The age of a first driver's license. The age of smiles without braces. The age of a first heartbreak.

"You know why we're here?" Uncle George asks me. I nod. "I have a new assignment for you, slave. This week I want you making friends with some of these young girls out here. We're going to come home with a bigger family then what we came with." The thought of bringing anyone else into this hell makes me dizzy. I don't think I can do it. I try to remember what it feels like to be innocent. These girls look so normal. They're happy. They have friends. Families. Dreams.

"I want you to bring at least one girl back with you tonight." Uncle George says.

"How am I supposed to make friends with one of them? I don't think they will want to come with me."

"You wanna turn all the tricks yourself? Or do you want to have a break? You'll figure it out. Unless you want me to tear you up before you even get started." He raises his eyebrows. "You remember what that's like, don't you?" he says, grabbing my forearm with both hands and pulling my skin forcefully in opposite directions, as if wringing out a wet towel. I remember the last time. I think I passed out because of the pain because I can't remember anything past to first two minutes. "Or has it been too long?" his smirk evolves into a sadistic smile. "Joe, show her how it's done."

"Come on, let's take a walk." Joe says. We walk around the campgrounds. There are horse trailers, trucks, and RVs everywhere. Young kids with ropes and cowboy boots are running around doing rope tricks. Teen girls are flirting with teen boys, and parents are busy or absent. Competitors range in age from four to forty. Dummy roping, team roping, barrel racing, calf-tying, even bronco and bull riding. It's a prime place for trade and a common place for meeting new people to barter and travel with. For families who rodeo, home is wherever you hang your hat at the end of the night. Hard labor is respected more than an education. School is optional but contributing financially or with material goods is mandatory. A teenage boy, in the eyes of a cowboy, is just two more working hands. No one cares whether you can read or write—many of the grown men and women in rodeo can't. That's life being raised in the saddle.

From a distance I hear a girl screaming. "I told you, Mom. I don't want to!"

"Damn it, Anna! You're so selfish! You can stay home by yourself then!"

"See that?" Joe asks. I look over. A girl about twelve or thirteen years old is arguing with her mother. "Wait until she storms off or her mom leaves her, then go up to her and talk to her. Tell her you know how she feels. Tell her that you don't get along with your mom either. Then ask her if she wants to hang out with us."

I should be damned to hell for even thinking about this. I know what they are going to do with her if I bring her back. And she's going to know too. She's going to hate me like I hate Joe. For the rest of her life, she will remember my face as the selfish bitch who tricked her into coming with us. I don't know if I can do it. But I can't say no. They will make an example of me by beating me up, raping me and still making me work the rodeo. There's no way Uncle George would let us leave without her. If I don't do it, Joe will. It would only make it worse for me and for her if I try to fight back.

I invite her to come and rodeo with us. She doesn't hesitate to follow me and trusts everything I say to her. She tells her mom she'll see her in a week and that's the end of it. God knows if she'll ever see her again.

*A photo of myself (around 15 years old)
and other girls at a hotel between rodeos*

"Good work there, slave. I told you it wouldn't take much to bring her in. You stay in the back of the trailer with her. Tonight you'll take her pictures." Joe says. "You remember how we started you? We are going to have some fun on the internet this evening. Tomorrow we'll start her on some real work. Let's hit the road."

I walk around back and step into the trailer. The young girl is sitting there on the bed, looking around. Now I know why Joe made me make the bed and clean up this morning. "This is really nice," she says.

"Yeah. It's okay." *This feels so wrong. She has no idea.* "Your mom's not going to worry about you being with us on the road for a few weeks?"

"Nah. I leave all the time with other people. Mom's always on the road, too. If there's a rodeo I want to be part of and she doesn't want to go, I just catch a ride with somebody else. She wanted me to go with her to some place up north to sell horses, anyway. I told her I didn't want to go. She was just going to have me stay home. The neighbors are there if I need them. Anyway, she'll be happy to have some time away from me. She always wants to spend time with her new boyfriend and I'm just in her way. I told her I wouldn't be back for a week or so. She probably won't be either."

"Yeah I understand. My mom has a boyfriend too. Well, she's married to him now, but she's so busy trying to make him happy she doesn't really worry much about me or what I'm doing, either. It's Anna, right? How old are you?"

"Yeah. Anna. I'll be thirteen in four months."

"Cool," I say, heat radiating throughout my face. *How can I even look her in the eye? I never should have said anything to her.* But you can't say no to people like Joe or Uncle George. He isn't the only one turning out girls at rodeos, especially the big ones. He's made it clear more than once that if he wanted to, he could sell us to someone else with a reputation for breaking bones, or worse, a midwestern cowboy known for buying non-compliant girls only to use them and throw their bodies in a cornfield somewhere to decompose. I guess there's no way to tell if he really has a rodeo connection to a homicidal rapist, but I wouldn't put anything past him. I've watched plenty of sex girls come and go from rodeo circuits.

I didn't ask for this. I shouldn't have to do their dirty work, but I don't make the rules. It's not my fault she was in the wrong place at the wrong time. If it wasn't me who brought her in, it would be Joe, and we would all pay for crossing Uncle George. God, help me! I can't keep thinking.

We arrive back at the ranch and Uncle George tells Anna that she will be staying with me. He and Joe follow us to the guest house. Joe sets up the computer. "Are you ready, slave?" he asks me. He is sixteen now. I look at him and see a sick look of satisfaction as he observes Anna's eyes, wide in fear and disbelief. My guts are screaming, "no!" but I comply.

"Yeah," I say.

He hands me the camera. "Just the basics. I'll be back with George for a little initiation in a few minutes, so don't waste any time."

Anna's squirming. Her eyes dart back and forth. She cracks her knuckles again and again, her foot bouncing rapidly. "Sorry Anna, I hate to do this, but I have to take your picture. I know you probably want to run, but let's face it—there's nowhere for you to go. You don't know anyone here where we are. I'm not making you do anything I haven't already done myself. Take it from me, it's easier if you don't fight. I've earned my share of beatings and trust me, it's not worth it." A chill runs down my back as I look down at the burn mark on my arm. I remember when I said 'no.' They burned me with a cattle prod that had been laying over a bed of coals. "There's some liquor in the cabinet if you want some," I offer her.

"I'm twelve. I don't drink."

"Well, that'll probably change." *I wish she hadn't reminded me.*

I take the pictures of Anna. Self-hatred burns so hot that it beckons suicide. I try not to think about what I am doing. The hope of being free has been gone so long that I don't even dream about escape anymore. I see myself through the lens, and with every flash of the camera I flash back to another special request from a revolting screenname like Dddy4U, $$forYNG, or DirtyOldMan. After the third click, time freezes and I almost drop the camera. I manage to catch it against my leg, jolting me back to the present before I turn into a sunflower. *That could have been really bad!*

Anna seems strong for her age. She's not crying, but I can tell by the way her eyes keep traveling back and forth that she can't wrap her head around this. "Don't try to make sense of it, you'll never be able to," I tell her.

"Why are you doing this?" she asks, "What is going to happen to me?"

"I don't have a choice, that's why. Someday you'll understand." *How did I get here? How am I sitting here having to take her pictures? I don't want to be here or do this. I just want to go home.*

Joe comes back into the room. He has me go onto the computer and log in to a teen chat site. The situation is all too familiar. Only this time, I am the one typing. A screen name is created. He's still using the same screenname: 2young4u, Uncle George's favorite screenname for attracting pedophiles.

97

As soon as I log in, chats fill up the screen. Grown men from their twenties to sixties all in a teen chat room looking for young girls. They tell us what they are looking for, and we create the scene for them. School girl. Father/daughter. Brother/sister. Teacher/student. Every imaginable forbidden sexual encounter. Most of the men have fantasies that include incest or rape. I learned quickly what they wanted, and Anna will learn too—act like you like what they are doing but cry enough for them to know that you don't. Be a good little girl but be bad too. Always say yes, but still beg them to stop.

They call us all kinds of names. Dirty whore. Bad bitch. Little girl. Stupid cunt. Some of them like to remind you that you aren't a real person. They'll call you a toy, a thing, or an it. Life feels a lot more like dying

when you don't have a name

or a bed

or a birthday

when you don't know what you like to eat

or wear

or do for fun

Your only purpose is to get them off and pretend like you like it. Well, except for the worst buyers.

The worst ones won't get off until they see you cry.

Uncle George walks into the room. "Slave," he says, "Come with me." He walks me to the trailer.

"I thought you said I was going to get a break?"

"You did get a break. But now you have to catch up." Uncle George laughs, holding the trailer door open with his dusty boot. He holds a cigarette between his lips and strikes a match. "You have five minutes," he mumbles.

Bringing Anna into the circle doesn't give me a break. We both have to work every day and every night. Looking at her is like watching what I had blocked out for so many years. I watch as her smile becomes a scowl, her eyes become a cesspool, and her once joyous laugh becomes mockery. I feel the heat of her hate for me burn against me like bare feet on blacktop. Every time we pass, I feel suffocated with guilt. My stomach bucks with intolerance to the acidic self-hatred that burns me from the inside, eating away at what's left of me.

I long for freedom

but

                  my freedom

presents itself

              as a noose

                        a bottle of pills

        or

the cold   hard   steel

              of a silver bullet,

              rather than a one-way ticket home.

When summer break is over Uncle George drives me to the airport. He doesn't have to tell me to be quiet anymore. He knows I won't say anything, and I know if I did no one would believe me. Most of the trip is made in complete silence. "Two more years and we won't have to make any more trips to the airport, eh slave? You'll travel with us and you can leave your past behind in Colorado. You won't have to worry about finding some place to go, huh?" He puts his hand on my leg and shakes it as if he's trying to get me excited about it.

"Yeah." I say.

It wouldn't be so bad if I didn't have to go back and forth. It always seems harder when I go back to Mom's because nothing I do is ever good enough for Alan. I don't want to live forever with Joe and Uncle George, but I'll never be able to get a place on my own. Mom has Alan, but I can tell he doesn't really want me around. He's just waiting for me to turn eighteen so I can leave and go to college, but I don't even think I will graduate high school. Maybe it would be better for me to stay at the ranch and travel for rodeos. I smile when I picture the loping horses. *I remember when I thought I was going to learn how to barrel race. I remember thinking about how good it would feel when I won. I know I would have been good at it. It just wasn't for me. I know what I am and what I will always be. A call girl. A whore. Just a worthless nothing. No one wants me but Joe and Uncle George. At least I know they have a place for me to live. I know what to expect when I'm with them. I may not be good at anything else, but at least I'm good at sex.*

Uncle George parks the truck and walks me to security. "See you at Christmas time," he says to me, tipping his cowboy hat at the security officer.

A photo of me at about 15 years old in the barn with a baby pig

LOSING KATE, PART VII

I'm not sure if I would have left Wyoming had I known it was the last time I would see Joe and Uncle George. Most people assume that I would want to get away from them if I had the chance, but I couldn't trust anyone. The only people I thought would help me, my own mother and aunt, had told me in no uncertain terms to keep quiet and not fight the inevitable. If they didn't care to help, nobody would. And anyway, after all these years, I'm used to the way things are. I'm comfortable because I know what to expect. And I know I deserve it. I know what I am. Things can always be worse, that's what Uncle George always says. Joe tells me I'm better off working for him. "We're family!" he says. "Nobody will take care of you like family will. You can't trust other people, they will tell you they care but at the end of the day they don't give a shit."

Joe is sure to remind me of my place and purpose in the world. But at least I *have* a purpose—even if it isn't the best kind, it's better than nothing at all. I know I can wake up each day and expect the same thing. I don't have to guess what is going to happen to me. I know. At the end of the night, no matter who I have been with, I know where I am going to end up—either in the trailer or on the ranch, and that is the closest thing to peace I can find. After everything I've been through, Uncle George and Joe have never left me. I can trust them.

Now I'm supposed to go back to school, but I can't stop thinking about Anna. *She was a normal kid and I messed her up. I wish I had never gone over to talk to her. She could have grown up to have a normal life—finish high school, go to college...but now she will never have that.* The worst part is that she is going to have to work year-round with Joe and Uncle George and I won't be able to stay and protect her. *She has so much to learn. I hope she will be okay.* Uncle George is such a smooth talker that he convinced Anna's mom to let him take her to rodeo competitions and said Aunt Lisa would homeschool her with Joe.

What If____Would Have Happened?

I can't tell you
how it might have been
I can't change what's taken place

but I can tell you what I've learned
to point you in the right direction:

In order to make a difference
you must hate evil
more than you fear rejection.

Stand up for what is right
Stand up to what is wrong
And understand that the road of recovery is
uncomfortably long.

What works today
may not work tomorrow
so be prepared to take steps back
it's not a sign of weakness
but a sign you are on track.

Ghost

I put my hand over my heart

                      but I can't feel

                                              anything

My therapist says

                    sometimes that happens

                                  when you are numb

I scratch my skin sometimes

                              to see   if I'm real

            when I watch   myself

and when I don't feel it

                    I know   it's just   a dream

My therapist asks me what happened to my arm

         and I ask her   if she believes   in ghosts

She says she believes   in something

                         but she isn't sure

so I rub   my arm

         and say,   "I do."

         She asks me again,   "What happened to your arm"

and I tell her,

                         "a ghost scratched it"

I crawl   under Mom's bed

                         because my cat likes to hide there

and   I need to know   if I am alive

I hear her   purring   but   it's   not
              enough

so   I put my hand   on her belly

         She hisses

                         and scratches the ghost

The cat runs   out   from under the bed

Mom runs   into the room   and screams

I hear booms

        and crashes

           he must be really angry

I   don't move

      because   I   don't   like   scary movies

and mom   is terrified   of ghosts

It's   a   l o n g   movie

    and   in the
end

      everyone   is crying

I missed   the bus

     so I change my shoes

the walk   is longer   than the
movie

The next day in homeroom class   Mrs. Jordan says,

    "It's nice of you to join us today."

110

but I'm not being nice

                              and neither is she.

I can't focus on anything in school anymore because everything reminds me

of something bad
and then   I turn into a sunflower.

It makes it really hard for me to know what's happening, so I forget a lot of things. Almost everyone gets frustrated at me and tells me I'm not listening or that I'm stupid,
but sunflowers
don't have ears.

It's **loud** inside my head. I have to make it quiet before I can hear someone talking to me. I can see their mouths move, but it takes me a minute before I can hear anything besides **noise**. Once I start to hear actual words, I just need them to **slow down**. If they slow down, I can follow what they are saying. But if they start to yell, I have to start all over again to quiet the noise on the inside.

Sometimes it helps me focus if I have something to hold in my hands. People make fun of me sometimes because I still play with playdoh and silly putty. It's sticky, and it helps me keep my head and my body together.

My body and my head don't like each other, so they try not to be in the same place at the same time. When the body leaves, my head will come back. And when the head leaves, I can't remember what happens with my body.

Some teachers keep asking if I am okay
(I'm not)
but if I said so
I would have to answer more questions
and I'm too tired

My report card from 10th grade: Unable to focus,
I was failing every class

My Body Can't Talk

I am missing my first period class
though I don't even realize it
as I grow cold,
wet with tears,
hood over my head,
legs pulled up underneath my sweatshirt
like a frightened child, afraid of the dark.

"Kate," she shouts
"Kate!" the teacher calls out my name
to demand I get to class
but I don't hear her.

My mind is stuck in the closet
of my grandparent's bathroom
with the door locked, crying
"Please don't"

"Kate, are you doing okay?" my teacher asks. "*Kate!!*"

I stare down at my hands and pick at the hangnails on my fingers.

"Kate, I am talking to you!" she shakes my shoulder, "Are you alright?"

"Huh? Ummm, yeah, fine." *Kate. Nobody has called me that in a long time.* Mom never calls me anything but "honey" or "baby," and she calls everybody that. *Kate.* I laugh aloud.

"Is something funny?" she asks. *Hardly. She has no idea who I am.*

"Is there something you want from me?"

"You're looking awfully gaunt," she says. "and it's a little warm for you to still be wearing sweats and a sweatshirt."

"I get cold easy," I say. *Gaunt? Good. Maybe I will slowly disappear and everyone will just leave me alone. What does she care about me anyway?*

"I've seen you sitting during the lunch hour. Do you ever eat lunch?"

"Yeah, I eat lunch." I lie. *Nobody wants to be with a scrawny woman.* I try to keep emotions from my face, but I'm relieved to know that I am getting smaller.

"Okay," she says.

I head out the door toward the stairwell to make my way to my next class. I get a sharp pain behind my eyes and they go blurry. I feel dizzy.

I wake up on a cot, surrounded by white walls. Nothing is familiar. I look down and panic when I realize they took off my sweatshirt.

"Where's my hoodie?!"

"We have it over here," the nurse says. "Why don't you sit up. Here. Eat this granola bar. You are looking very pale." The nurse says.

"Um, no thanks. I'm not hungry."

"I didn't ask if you were hungry. Eat it. You passed out, it could very likely be from low blood sugar."

"I don't want it." Her eyes narrow as she looks at me.

"How about you step over here so I can get your height and weight."

"Do I really have to do that?"

"Yes. I would like to write your information in your report here." I slip off the cot and stand against the wall.

"5'2" she says. "Now, step on the scale please." I step on the scale. "Seventy-nine pounds. That's hardly substantial for a high school student, don't you think, Kate?" I shrug. She picks up the phone and dials a number.

"Hello, is this Kate's mother? Yes, I am going to need you to come to the school and pick her up. She passed out not too long ago, and we need you to take her in for a physical and psychological checkup before she returns to school. We'll need the results before she returns to classes."

After I was sent home from school, a report was filed to the Department of Child Welfare. After an investigation, it was determined that I could not stay at home and recommended that I receive intensive care in a residential treatment facility. I was sent to another state to the first of many residential treatment facilities, where I stayed until I ran away, just before my eighteenth birthday. It was the beginning of a long, difficult, and worthwhile journey—one that has yet to be written.

A hospital bracelet from when I was admitted at 15
for an eating disorder and severe dissociative episodes

The road to recovery has no end

Only new beginnings

ACKNOWLEDGEMENTS

My partner—for encouraging me to put this book together and supporting me every step of the way. You have loved me through my ugliest moments. Your arms, always open to hold me and your loving hand to lift my chin when my head is weighed down with shame.

My ray of hope—Arrayah Claire, for giving me a reason to be brave.

Lizz Alezetes—for pushing me to be a better writer—this book is better because of you. Not only have you been a phenomenal editor, but you have also become a friend.

Jessa Crisp--for allowing me to use your photo on the cover of my book. What you captured is symbolic to me in my recovery.

Twin—for making sure I'm never alone and for being the one person who really gets me. From the womb to the grave.

My ride-or-die's—Kristy Cox, Savannah Sanders, and Kimberly Grabert for loving and supporting me throughout my journey, in times where I didn't think I could keep going.

Poppy—for your hard work, commitment and dedication which empowered our family and changed history for Chicanos everywhere.

Mom—for having the courage to face the truth and acknowledge it, no matter how difficult. Thank you for supporting me when I decided to speak out as an adult and not trying to filter my message or my truth.

Kris and Bobby—for being the best future in-laws a person could ask for and for enriching Arrayah's life as grandparents. You've both taught me so much about resilience and hard work.

Elizabeth Scaife—for your hard work in the anti-trafficking movement. For seeing me and hearing me that day I wandered into a training you did in my town. You saw my pain before I could fully acknowledge it and you invited me into your circle that provided me the support I needed to heal. Your faith has filled me with hope and your friendship has filled my belly with baleadas.

Bonnie Martin, Kristen Tenuta, Katie Raines, Kristina Haus, and Tracy McDaniel—for being the best therapists of the 25+ counselors I have tried in my lifetime.

My service dog, PTS-Deetz, for your unconditional love and commitment to improve my health. You are my destiny dog, Deetz Destino.

Morgan Rumple and Kate Kimmer for really getting it, always being real, and supporting me. Your boldness and commitment pave the way to freedom for more lives than you will ever know. Our friendship is a soul connection—you have given me a safe place to be vulnerable. You give me grace when I am ignorant and are humble enough to teach me but honest enough to laugh with me about it. You challenge me to be a better person and to be self-aware. You are every bit as worthy of the same fight you put up for others.

Stephanie Holt—thank you for being a true friend. Your passion, humility, faith and boldness inspire me always. Your commitment to being yourself is refreshing and inspiring. Eres mi amiga para siempre, la salvadoreña de mi corazón.

Katrina Mallory, Eliza Reock, and Morgan Bow—thank you for always going above and beyond in the work that you do, and yet always finding the time to answer the phone when I call.

Minette Valentine-Kamara—your brave and your advocacy is the kind that changes the world.

Eric Harris—for being the big brother I always wanted and Heather Helbig, his sidekick, and my friend.

Andrea Marie Varty—I love you and I miss you. I think of you every day.

Tammy Turon—for the incredible difference you have made in my life and for loving and caring unconditionally.

Mrs. Ford—my world history teacher, who cared enough to see that I was not okay and to speak up about it—I have no idea if you'll ever see this, but your small acts of kindness and your bravery to speak out saved my life.

Mrs. Brener, my high school social worker and the school nurse, whose name I never knew—for playing an instrumental role in getting me the help I needed.

Samantha Floyd—for setting an example that challenges me to speak louder about injustice, call out oppression, and acknowledge my privilege. I didn't know how silent I was until I heard you speak up so loudly.

My pen pal—Dura, April Arnold for being a bright spot during seasons of depression.

My CITC staff who loved me when I needed it most.

Sarah, Ben, Kate, Brittany, Justin, Kacey, Britt, Tasia, and BK—I couldn't have survived without you.

Kathy Dirschell and Pat McAfee—for taking me in and adopting me as your grandkid when I desperately needed that love, care and support—and for remaining in my life through all of its turbulence.

Andy Gibson—for inspiring me to pick up a pen and a microphone again to heal through poetry.

Indianapolis poets—you know who you are. For giving me a safe space to embrace myself without fear (special shoutout to VOCAB).

Tim McClain--for all of your help with tech and photography. And for the kind of friendship where we can business ideas while watching *Goosebumps*.

Jen Spry--I have never vibed so closely with someone I had so many opposing view with. Our friendship is one of a kind and one that will last forever.

Jennifer Kempton—for raising hell on earth for justice when you lived, and for raising hell on earth for justice when you passed.

All of my Survivor Siblings, too many to mention—we couldn't do this without one another.

All those whose lives have been cut short because of injustice—you are the reason we keep on fighting.

And to Hope—the day you left me was the most painful day I have ever endured. Not a day goes by that I don't think of you. You saved me. I did everything I knew how to save you.

NOTES

1 McCleeland, D., & Gilyard, C. (n.d.) Phoenix Society for Burn Survivors. "Calming Trauma—How Understanding the Brain Can Help." https://www.phoenix-society.org/resources/entry/calming-trauma-how-understanding-the-brain-can-help

[2] Lennon, J., & McCartney, P. (1968). "Blackbird" (song) from the album *The Beatles*.

[iii] Finkelhor, D. (2012). "Characteristics of Crimes against Juveniles." Crimes against Children Research Center.

[iv] David, M., Hoffman, A., Livingston, J. (1950). "A Dream is a Wish Your Heart Makes." From the album *Cinderella* (1950 film soundtrack).

For more information about K.D. Roche you can visit www.kdroche.com or join their quarterly listserv by request via email: info@kdroche.com

You can book K.D. as a keynote speaker, trainer or consultant you can email them at info@kdroche.com or visit their website.